D1475837

Eleanor Roosevelt
First Lady and Civil Rights Activist

written by Darlene R. Stille   illustrated by Reed Sprunger

Beginner Biographies

Content Consultant:
Victoria Grieve, PhD
Department of History, Utah State University

magic wagon

visit us at www.abdopublishing.com

Published by Magic Wagon, a division of the ABDO Group, PO Box 398166, Minneapolis, MN 55439. Copyright © 2013 by Abdo Consulting Group, Inc. International copyrights reserved in all countries. All rights reserved. No part of this book may be reproduced in any form without written permission from the publisher.

Looking Glass Library™ is a trademark and logo of Magic Wagon.

Printed in the United States of America, North Mankato, Minnesota.
092012
012013

Text by Darlene R. Stille
Illustrations by Reed Sprunger
Edited by Holly Saari
Series design and cover production by Emily Love
Interior production by Craig Hinton

Library of Congress Cataloging-in-Publication Data

Stille, Darlene R.
  Eleanor Roosevelt : first lady and civil rights activist / written by Darlene R. Stille ; illustrated by Reed Sprunger.
     p. cm. – (Beginner biographies)
  Includes index.
  ISBN 978-1-61641-941-7
1. Roosevelt, Eleanor, 1884-1962–Juvenile literature. 2. Civil rights workers–United States–Biography-
-Juvenile literature. 3. Women civil rights workers–United States–Biographpy–Juvenile literature. 4.
Presidents' spouses–United States–Biography–Juvenile literature. I. Sprunger, Reed, ill. II. Title.
  E807.1.R48S74 2013
  973.917092–dc23
  [B]
                        2012023801

Table of Contents

Little Nell

Eleanor Roosevelt was born on October 11, 1884, in New York City. Her parents named her Anna Eleanor, but most people called her Eleanor. Her father, Elliot, called her Little Nell. Eleanor loved her father. He made her laugh.

Eleanor's mother, Anna, was very beautiful. Next to her mom, Eleanor thought of herself as ugly. Anna called her daughter "Granny." She thought the little girl acted too old-fashioned.

Eleanor's father would throw her up in the air and catch her.

Eleanor served food to the newspaper boys.

The Roosevelts were a big family. Eleanor had many aunts, uncles, and cousins. Most of her relatives were wealthy. Eleanor soon learned that not everyone lived the way she did. There were many poor children in New York City. Eleanor's grandfather had started a home for poor boys who sold newspapers. Her father sometimes took her to help out at the home.

Eleanor never forgot the experience of helping the poor newspaper boys. It was the first of many times she would help those in need.

An Orphan

When Eleanor was eight years old, her mother died. Eleanor went to live with her grandmother, who was stern and strict. Her father was unable to care for her because he was sick. Two years later, he died. At age ten, Eleanor was an orphan.

Eleanor loved to visit her Uncle Teddy and Aunt Edith. They lived in a big house on Long Island, New York. Uncle Teddy had big teeth and round glasses. Eleanor loved her jolly uncle. He called Eleanor his favorite niece.

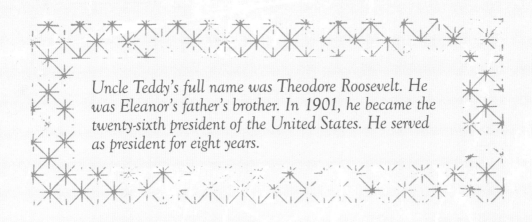

Uncle Teddy's full name was Theodore Roosevelt. He was Eleanor's father's brother. In 1901, he became the twenty-sixth president of the United States. He served as president for eight years.

Eleanor read with her Uncle Teddy.

Eleanor went to a school for girls in England when she was 15 years old. Eleanor thought it was a wonderful place! She was a good student. Many of her teachers and classmates liked her.

After high school graduation, Eleanor returned to New York City. She started working with social reform groups. These helped women and poor people have better lives.

Eleanor got along well with her classmates and teachers.

11

Eleanor and Franklin
lived in New York City
after they married.

Marriage and Family

In 1902, Eleanor met Franklin Roosevelt. He was a distant cousin of hers. After some time, they fell in love. He asked Eleanor to marry him, and she said yes. They did not know it, but their marriage would change the world.

Franklin and Eleanor were married in New York City on March 17, 1905. They had six children. Eleanor tried to be a good wife and mother.

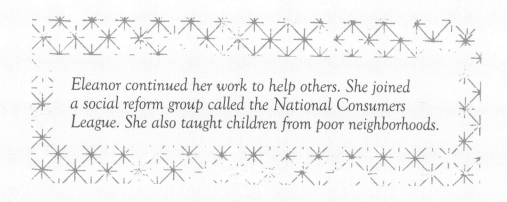

Eleanor continued her work to help others. She joined a social reform group called the National Consumers League. She also taught children from poor neighborhoods.

When Eleanor married Franklin, many changes were happening in the world. Women were trying to get the right to vote. Working people were trying to get paid more.

Eleanor told Franklin about these things. Throughout her life, Eleanor would often bring important issues to Franklin's attention. Then, he would help bring changes through his job in politics.

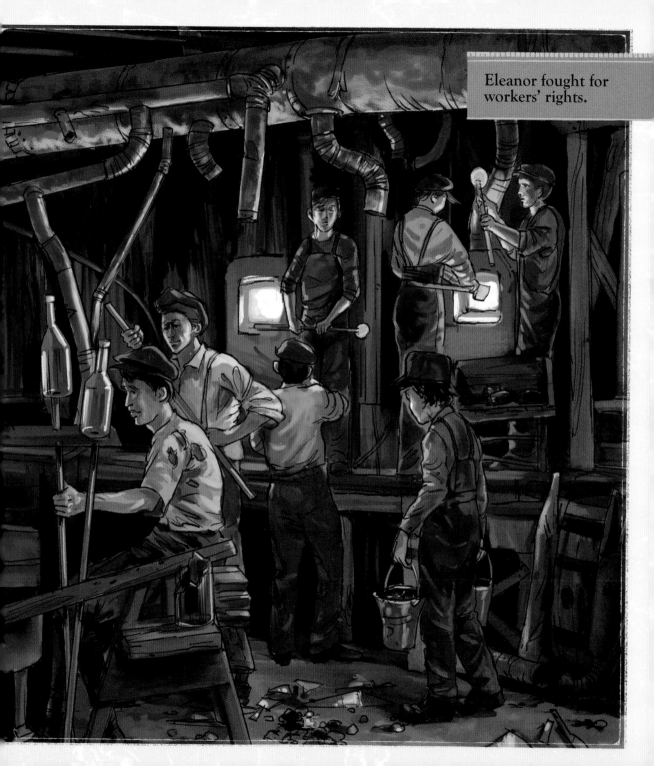

Eleanor fought for workers' rights.

Eleanor stayed active with public service after moving to Washington DC.

Public Service

In 1910, Franklin was elected a New York state senator. Eleanor packed up her family and moved to Albany, the state capital.

It was not long before Eleanor had to move her family again. This time they moved to Washington DC, the capital of the United States. Eleanor met and talked with many important people during this time. She also kept working for schools in New York City.

Then in 1914, World War I broke out in Europe. In 1917, Eleanor began working for the Red Cross. She went overseas to help take care of wounded soldiers and sailors.

Eleanor loved her work. After the war, she visited battlefields. She saw farms and towns in ruins. She thought wars were a terrible idea. She believed countries needed a better way to work out their problems.

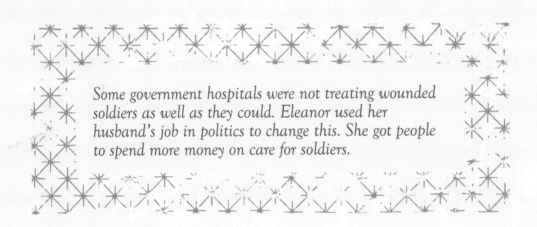

Some government hospitals were not treating wounded soldiers as well as they could. Eleanor used her husband's job in politics to change this. She got people to spend more money on care for soldiers.

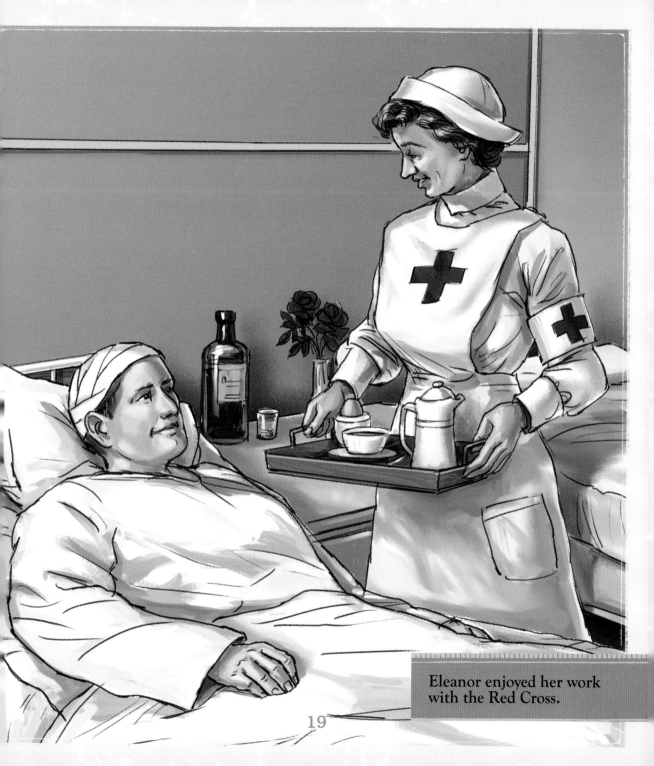

Eleanor enjoyed her work
with the Red Cross.

19

Eleanor was a strong supporter of women's rights. She joined the League of Women Voters. This group helped gain women's right to vote. Eleanor also worked to make women's jobs safe and healthy.

In 1921, Eleanor's life took a challenging turn. Franklin developed polio. The disease damaged his legs badly, and he had to use a wheelchair. Eleanor took a more active role in politics to help her husband. She talked with people about their problems and needs.

Women's rights were very important to Eleanor.

Life as First Lady

In 1933, Franklin was sworn in as president. Eleanor became First Lady of the United States. In the past, a First Lady's main duty had been to host parties. Eleanor did not want to do that. Instead, she wanted to continue her work helping others.

The country had big problems. Many people were out of work. Very few jobs existed. Families lost their farms and homes. Eleanor visited people all around the country. She and Franklin believed the government should help them.

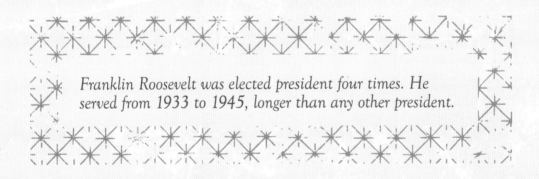

Franklin Roosevelt was elected president four times. He served from 1933 to 1945, longer than any other president.

As First Lady, Eleanor lived in the White House in Washington DC.

Eleanor became a new kind of First Lady. She made speeches and held meetings. She wrote a newspaper column called "My Day." Eleanor also had a radio show. Soon, many people in the country knew who Eleanor Roosevelt was. But sometimes they didn't like her views.

In 1939, African-American singer Marian Anderson was turned away from singing at a building. The group that owned the building would not let her perform because she was an African American. Eleanor was a member of the group. She learned of how the group treated Anderson. Eleanor quit the group to protest their racist actions.

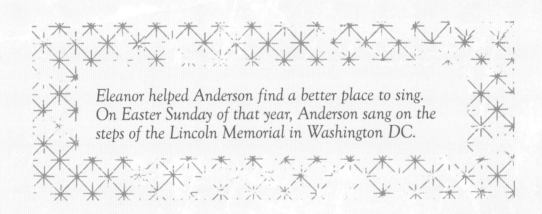

Eleanor helped Anderson find a better place to sing. On Easter Sunday of that year, Anderson sang on the steps of the Lincoln Memorial in Washington DC.

Anderson sang in front of 75,000 people at the Lincoln Memorial.

At the United Nations, Eleanor worked with people from different countries.

Working for Rights

In 1941, the United States entered World War II. Eleanor visited soldiers and sailors all over the world. Franklin became ill during the war. He died in 1945. Eleanor was very sad to lose her husband.

Eleanor was no longer First Lady. But the new president, Harry S. Truman, had plans for her. He sent her to work for a group called the United Nations. Many countries joined this group. Eleanor worked with them to help end wars.

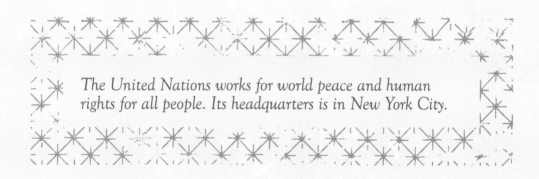

The United Nations works for world peace and human rights for all people. Its headquarters is in New York City.

Eleanor believed all people should be treated fairly, no matter what they looked like or where they came from. She helped write the Universal Declaration of Human Rights. It said that every person in the world was born with certain rights that could not be taken away.

Eleanor died on November 7, 1962, at age 78. She had spent her life working for ordinary people. She helped minorities gain equal rights. She helped poor people. She became one of the best known women in the world. Eleanor lived a life to be proud of.

Eleanor worked hard to help write the Universal Declaration of Human Rights.

FUN FACTS

+ Eleanor Roosevelt was the first First Lady to fly in an airplane.

+ The home of Eleanor Roosevelt, Val-Kill in Hyde Park, New York, is the only National Historic Site that honors a First Lady.

+ Eleanor and Franklin Roosevelt had several Scottish terriers as pets. The most famous was Fala.

+ Eleanor Roosevelt was the first First Lady to hold press conferences for women reporters only.

TIMELINE

1884 Anna Eleanor Roosevelt was born on October 11 in New York City.

1899 Eleanor began attending a school for girls in England.

1905 On March 17, Eleanor married Franklin Roosevelt.

1917 Eleanor worked with the Red Cross to help soldiers and sailors during World War I.

1921 Eleanor became more active in politics after Franklin got polio.

1933 Eleanor became First Lady of the United States.

1941 Eleanor visited many soldiers and sailors during World War II.

1945 Eleanor began working for the United Nations.

1948 The Universal Declaration of Human Rights, which Eleanor helped write, was adopted by the United Nations.

1962 Eleanor died on November 7.

GLOSSARY

battlefield—the place were a battle is fought.

declaration—an announcement.

equal rights—the rights of people to be treated with equal respect as all others.

minority—a smaller group of people, often not treated equally with the larger group of people.

politics—the affairs having to do with getting elected and running the government.

protest—to object to or speak out against something.

racist—having the belief that one race is better than another.

social reform—the activities that work to change parts of society.

universal—something that applies to all people everywhere.

LEARN MORE

At the Library

Amnesty International. *We Are All Born Free*. London: Frances Lincoln Publishers, 2008.

Cooney, Barbara. *Eleanor*. New York: Viking, 1999.

Ryan, Pam Muñoz. *When Marian Sang: The True Recital of Marian Anderson: The Voice of a Century*. New York: Scholastic, 2002.

On the Web

To learn more about Eleanor Roosevelt, visit ABDO Group online at **www.abdopublishing.com**. Web sites about Roosevelt are featured on our Book Links page. These links are routinely monitored and updated to provide the most current information available.

INDEX